NEW ENGLAND FOLIAGE TRAILS...

by Jay Woodard

Published by Anglo-American Publishing Co.

Published by Anglo-American Publishing Co.
  P.O. Box 5009-151
  Sugar Land, Texas 77478
Copyright© 1988 by Jay Woodard
All Rights Reserved
First Edition — June, 1988
Typesetting & Layout by Type Connection
  Houston, Texas
Printed by Paramount Printing Co. Ltd.
Printed in Hong Kong
ISBN: 0-9618888-2-2
Library Of Congress Catalog Number 88-70887

New England Foliage Trails is dedicated to my family, friends, and business associates (both in and out of the publishing business) who encouraged me in my endeavor.

This book is also dedicated, with their permission, to Governor John B. Connally and his lovely wife, Nellie. Their courage in facing life's hardest challenges has been an inspiration to me and countless others.

Introduction

Since I was very young, I have been fascinated by photographs of New England in the autumn. One of my earliest goals in life was to someday go there and see the wondrous beauty in person. Unfortunately, I never made it while growing up, but still the goal remained. After getting married in 1970, I told my wife every year, "this is my New England year". It seems my plans were always put off until the next year, then the next, and the next.

Finally, in the late summer of 1987, I started the yearning again. Only this time, I had a definite purpose for going. A few months earlier I had published my first book, <u>Texas Bluebonnet Trails</u> a photograph book on the state flower of Texas. The experience of doing my first book had been one of the most rewarding experiences of my life. So I began to look for another book to do. The idea for this New England book seemed a natural second selection. The more I thought about it, the more excited I became. So, one evening, I came home from work and told Carole, my wife, that I had actually booked the flight—to Boston. Nothing could stop me now—I was leaving on October 15! My two kids, Jill and Jayson, just shrugged me off, as it to say, "There goes dad on another of his crazy mid-life adventures."

Continued next page...

Flying to Boston, I suddenly realized that I knew very little about the area into which I was heading. I did have a map, showing all six New England States—Maine, New Hampshire, Vermont, Connecticutt, Massachusetts, and Rhode Island. That's all the planning I had done in advance, other than arrange for a compact rental car to be ready for me at the Boston airport. I had all my camera gear packed in a suitcase. It consisted of one camera (a ten-year-old Canon AE-1, with no flash), a 28 mm—85 mm Vivitar zoom lens, a twenty-five-year-old tripod, and lots of Kodachrome 64 slide film.

Once in Boston, I picked up my rental car at the airport and asked the lady at the desk how to get to the road that would go north, up the coast of Maine. She pointed me in the right direction and I was off.

For the next six days I managed to cover just under 2,000 miles of beautiful New England. Traveling down a highway, I would glimpse a scene, pull off, get the best angle and take a shot. Many times I would turn blindly onto a country lane and just follow it, stopping at river crossings, wooded hillsides, and villages along the way. Luckily, I never had a problem finding a place to stay for the night. The local people were friendly and helpful wherever I went.

You may notice I have not given the locations of the photographs used in this book. I felt that would take away from the fact that beauty like this is throughout New England in the fall. Besides, the scenes will never look the same year after year.

The accompanying verses were selected because I felt they helped accentuate the mood of each photograph.

This book has been a joy to produce. I sincerely hope you will enjoy it.

—Jay Woodard

The Author's Path of Leaves Resplendent

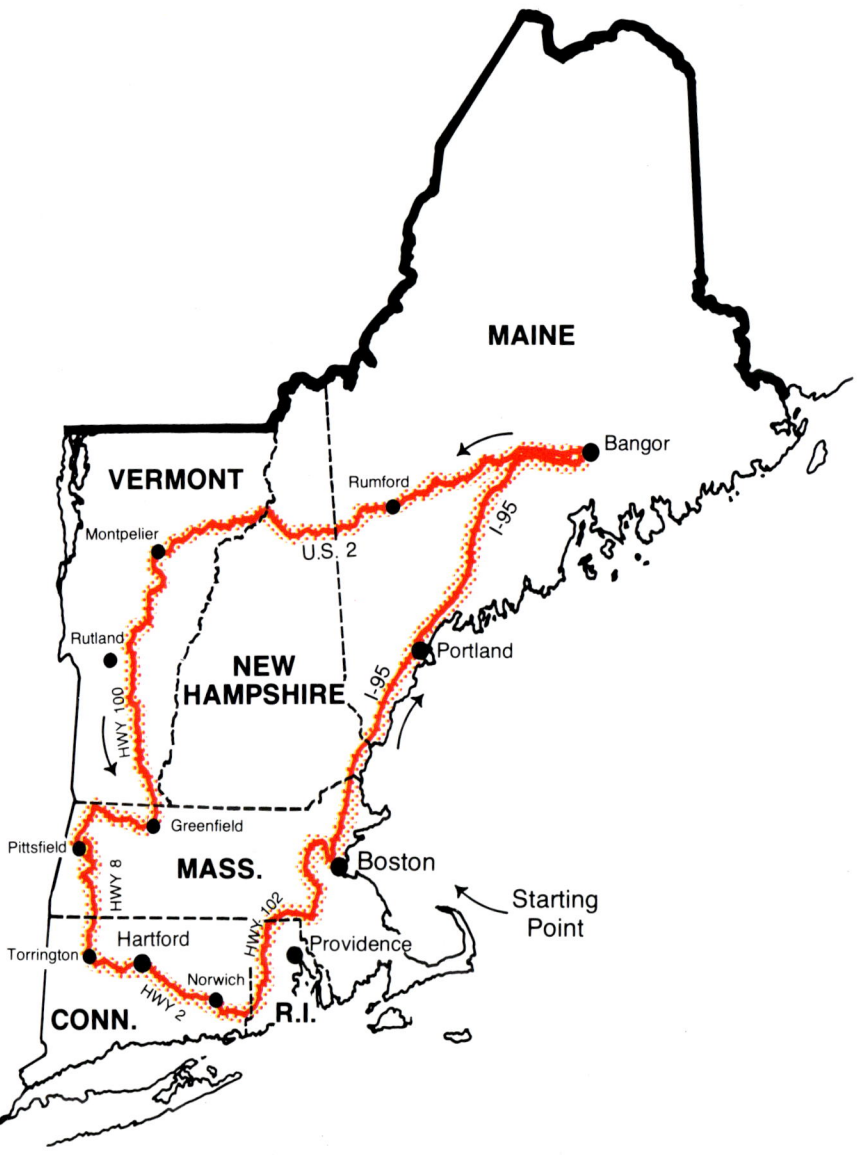

Map by Taffa-Graphics
Houston, Texas

MAINE

VERMONT

Bangor

Rumford

Montpelier

U.S. 2

I-95

NEW HAMPSHIRE

Rutland

HWY 100

Portland

I-95

Greenfield

Pittsfield

MASS.

Boston

HWY 8

HWY 102

Hartford

Providence

Starting Point

Torrington

Norwich

R.I.

HWY 2

CONN.

The placid shade of the October woods brings a calm to our souls. The breezes that make the leaves flutter bring a healing to our languid thoughts of bygone days.
—Michele Sharojan

One touch of nature makes the whole world kin.
                                        —*Shakespeare*

Autumn is the American season. In Europe the leaves turn yellow or brown, and fall. Here they take fire on the trees and hang there flaming. We think this frost-fire is a portent somehow: a promise that the continent has given us. Life, too, we think, is capable of taking fire in this country; of creating beauty never seen.

—Archibald MacLeish

Enchantment can be found on every village street. The green leaves mature into nature's finest jewels. The simplest scenes take on a glorious splendor and beg us to stay as we go reverently on our way.

—*Libil Pitts*

The hollow echo, as we trotted through the covered bridge, brought back ghosts of past generations.

—Barbara Stephens

The day is cold, and dark, and dreary;
It rains, and the wind is never weary;
The vine still clings to the mouldering wall,
But at every gust the dead leaves fall,
And the day is dark and dreary.

—*Longfellow*

7

*Colors splash across the landscape, and footsteps rustle
through the serene New England woods - our hearts are full
with the wealth and glory of the year.*

—Charles Ronfill

The solemn stillness of our melancholy days, fenced in by autumn, gives time for quiet meditation.

— David Lynwood

Ah, a dream of perfect bliss! The wind's deep symphony sighs that this beauty is truly God's handwriting.

— *Dr. Pat Melstaff*

Autumn has passed this way once more, leaving us a legacy to last another year.

—Marie Artfrey

Come with me, and let us seek together our memories along the autumn lane. Who knows what treasures we might find among the colors there. For I'll be there to hold your hand and bring to mind those pleasant times of long ago.
— *Brenda Terive Laurles*

Meditate on the creation before you—for surely it is the face of God.

—Floyd Salreese

While October's trees rock stiffly, adorned in their coats of aging leaves, the old house just sits and waits—for better days? for a peaceful end? And we can only watch and appreciate the mysterious beauty of the ghosts of autumns past.

—Claye Hollylance

15

Simple things in life form more permanent pictures in our memories...an idle autumn breeze on the lane, splashed with the color of the season, the postman's mail car rustling up the hill...

—Don Jocelyn

Do not think of your faults; still less of others' faults; in every person who comes near you look for what is good and strong: honor that; rejoice in it; and, as you can, try to imitate it; and your faults will drop off, like dead leaves, when their time comes.

—*Ruskin*

To every thing there is a season, and a time to every purpose
under the heaven: A time to be born, and a time to die...
—*Old Testament, Ecclesiastes*

O World, I cannot hold thee close enough!
  Thy winds, thy wide grey skies!
  Thy mists, that roll and rise!
Thy woods, this autumn day, that ache and sag
And all but cry with colour...
  Lord, I do fear
Thou'st made the world too beautiful this year.
                      —*Edna St. Vincent Millay*

Like leaves on the race of man is found,
Now green in youth, now with'ring on the ground:
Another race the following spring supplies,
They fall successive and successive rise.

—Homer

The place seems to be waiting in the autumn stillness. For summer has grown weary and gone away in a whimper. Now the harvest season quietly tiptoes in on misty wings and spreads them gently over the tranquil village.
—Jo Ann Davereng

The autumn dream was ecstacy—it could not last...
It did not last. But...memories are our treasures here on earth.
—Doris O. Arthur

October smiled on New England's rivers, and scattered colors from the Artist's palette along their wooded banks.
—Jane Ann Ronstrum

Trees of splendor lined the city's streets. It was a time for remembering our childhood evenings there and the promises we made in crisp October breezes.

—*Robert Holt Linworth*

Like a country gate that's always open, welcoming all who wander by, our hearts are open to a faith that calms and stills.

—Mary Royford

The beauty of an autumn lane is like the memory of a lovely song.

—Ashley Russell

Through trees of splendor, the little stream rippled through visionary tints of fallen leaves.

— Pat Dalene Cherrice

An early snow surprised the autumn paradise...

*During the long shivering night God came here and
laid his gentle hand upon the earth.*

—*James Reese Harris*

*The autumn/winter scene calls to us. Share this moment
with me. It will be ours for all eternity.*

—Earl Wesley Taylor

The tints of autumn—a mighty flower garden blossoming under the spell of the enchanter, Frost.

—*Whittier*

32

When I saw the autumn landscape with fresh fallen snow, I put the window down and went back to bed. What a wonderful time of year!
—Wanda Glyn Ashbyhead

*The tranquil music of the stream soothes the autumn scene
overlaid with snow.*

—Mary Marcia Wayne

The day becomes more solemn and serene
  When noon is past: there is a harmony
  In Autumn, and a lustre in its sky
Which through the Summer is not heard or seen,
As if it could not be, as if it had not been!
                                    —*Shelly*

The heavens declare the glory of God, and the firmament sheweth his handywork.

—*Old Testament, Psalms, XIX, I*

October's snow of the foregoing day had covered the town. Our footsteps crunched their way toward the inn and we heard the joyous chatter of children coming from within. I smiled to myself as we stepped upon the porch, for I knew instinctly this would be our refuge as we journeyed through our autumn pilgrimage.

—B.D. Montgomery

I saw old Autumn in the misty morn
Stand shadowless like silence, listening
To silence.

—*Thomas Hood*

At the lake I can be still, and watch autumn in her passing.
— *Valjer B. Jeniki*

The little robin sat quite still in the back garden, seemingly disoriented by the unexpected blending of the two seasons.

—*Alan Sharish*

...then the snow was gone, just as softly as it had come.

Their work is almost finished now. Thus begins the natural process of decay and the graceful surrender of life.

—*Doris Harry*

There is something in the autumn that is native to my blood—
Touch of manner, hint of mood;
And my heart is like a rhyme,
With the yellow and the purple and the crimson keeping time.
                                                    —*Bliss Carman*

The simple autumn beauty of a New England red barn is etched into my memory like a mystical song.

— *Lee A. Robbins*

Boughs are daily rifled by the gusty thieves,
And the Book of Nature getteth short of leaves.
—Thomas Hood

The old red door, from its hinges fallen, lies among the wind scattered leaves of our Indian Summer.

— Florence Karmail

We had many a fine meal here, cooked outside in the crisp October air.

—Joan B. Franks

In all ranks of life the human heart yearns for the beautiful; and the beautiful things that God makes are his gift to all alike.

—*H.B. Stowe*

To be alive at this time, in this place —
to bear witness to the season's final act —
I am, indeed, a most fortunate recipient
of the Master's work.

                              Cormac Scoote Mitchell

Rather than following the beaten path through the autumn woods, we shall avoid it, and leave behind our own trail so that others may follow us. So it should be throughout our lives.

—Joan Ripwood

The governor stood in the leaf-filled gutter, admiring the capitol's beauty. The leaves crumbled and crunched as he walked slowly back and forth. He gazed studiously at the building as if he were a photographer trying to locate the perfect angle.

—Phillip K. Alowsky

52

Though we travel the world over to find the beautiful,
we must carry it with us or we find it not.
                                        —*Ralph Waldo Emerson*

The stately house stood silently among wind scattered leaves. It was at that moment I knew the meaning of Indian Summer.

— Alidean P. Chrisard

Oh, the sweet freshness of our quiet moments - we sit by the tranquil stream watching the leaves float gently to the ground.

—*Helen P. Alfred*

Time! Let this fall last a little longer—or
make it be less elegant.

—Laura Scott

Those who are addicted to Summer's folly are never quite at peace with themselves as those who can appreciate the beauty of each passing season.
—*Jean Nick-Lloyd*